MAGICAL TREEHOUSE
WORD & ART IN CAHOOTS!

www.MagicalTreehouse.com

Todd Henderson & James McNulty

Please come and meet this chap,
his name is Troy the Trog.
Troy lives in a deep damp cave
above a vulgar bog.

When you ask him what he is,
he says, “Caveman me finks.”
When you ask about the bog,
he says, “Me finks it stinks!”

Troy is also quick to say,
“Bog keeps Troy Trog alive.
Pesky dinos don’t come close
with teef as sharp as knives.”

But Troy the Trog is mighty bored
sitting round his cave.
The time has come to see new things
yet knows he must be brave.

Looking out, he takes a slip,
falls and cannot stop.
Toward the bog this Trog flies,
a short and sudden drop.

Landing onto something hard,
he gives a quick tap.
An echo then resounds from it,
like a hollow gap.

Then our Trog feels himself
going for a ride.
With a sudden scary jolt,
he's on a scaly slide!

As he lands he looks up
to see the saddest eyes.
“A baby dino needs me help,”
an unforeseen surprise.

"Pretty please, will you help?
I slipped off that wet log.
When I fell to the ground,
I landed in this bog!"

Troy is scared of dinosaurs,
yet says, "What rotten luck!
Me can't ignore a baby
with it's feet so very stuck!"

Troy knows he must act fast,
there's no time to stop!
He makes his way to a tree,
giving it a chop.

The tree cracks, creaks and sways,
crashing to the floor.
It lands between the baby
and those waiting at the shore.

“Come on dinos, now’s the time,
sink your teeth right in!
Pull this baby back to land
or she will sink not swim.”

"Quick! Bite each other's tails,
you must form a chain."
They tug and pull the baby in
like a chugging train.

A banner saying, "We love Troy!"
welcomes him ashore.
There's no time to celebrate,
here comes a CARNIVORE!

"Fear not Troy, now's our chance
to return the favour.
You're our friend, but to him,
Trog's a juicy flavour!"

The dinos start to gather round
and form a giant wall.
No carnivore stands a chance
against a wall so tall.

“Stay away!” One dino cries,
from the wall so strong.
Troy is now one of them
and feels that he belongs.

The spinosaurus comes and scowls,
"Trog looks yummy meat.
I promise to eat every bit,
even cheesy feet."

A huge tail rises up
and cracks just like a whip.
The spinosaurus runs and cries,
just caught by the tip.

“Fankoo my fine dino friends,
you surely saved me skin.”

Troy's not keen on being munched
by a beast like him!

A dino says, “By this bog,
is food we must keep near.
Yet with the bog always comes
a little dose of fear.”

"When we're stuck it is hard
to get back on land.
We're not scared of carnivores,
their teeth we can withstand."

"If you help when we fall,
we will rest with ease.
Then we'll help you come and go
as and when you please."

"Of course," says a smiling Trog,
he's super keen in fact.
Shaking hands and massive paws,
they form a solid pact.

From that day forth, Troy the Trog
did not sit round his cave.

Instead he makes the most of life,
so glad that he was brave.

Question Time...

1 - Do you think you could be friends with Troy the Trog?

2 - Would you like to live in Troy the Trog's cave?

3 - If you were Troy the Trog, would you be brave and look for new adventures?
Why?

4 - What do you think Troy the Trog eats?

5 - Have you ever helped someone and been helped in return?
Why do you think that is?

6 - Did you notice anything in the bog when Troy was looking out from his cave?

For more books by Todd & James, please visit...

www.MagicalTreehouse.com/books

Only Oscar! Full Collection

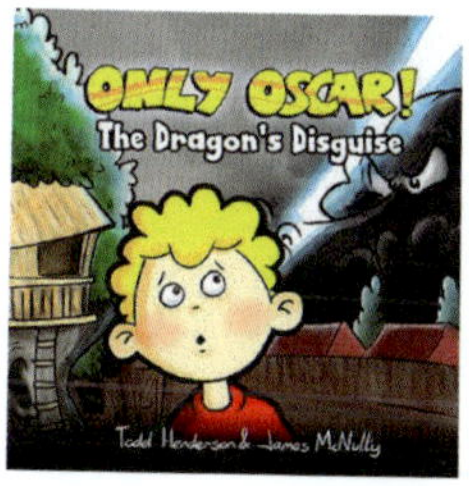

The Dragon's Disguise

A Storm is the Norm

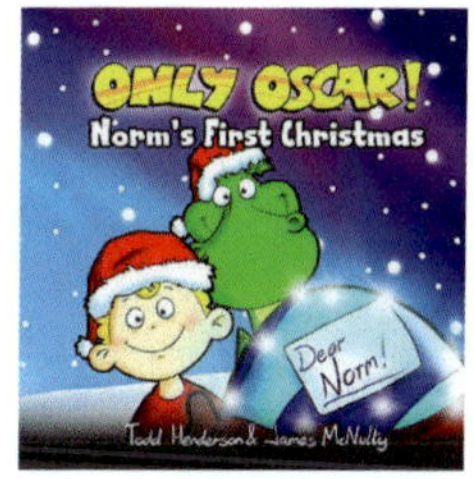

Norm's First Christmas

Back to School

Father's Day

Halloween

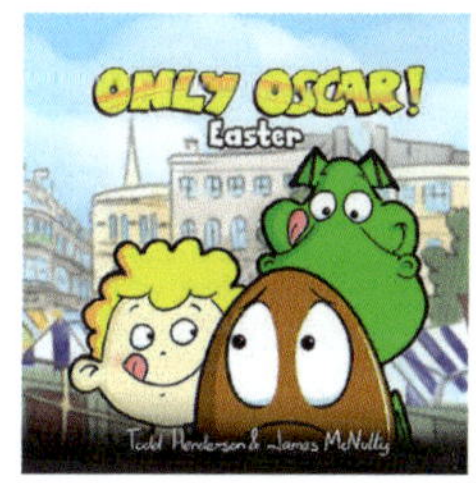

Easter

Other Titles...

The Unicorn with a

Unique Horn!

The Boggle Eyed Gog

Ugly Pugly &

Pigly Winks

Troy the Trog

TROY THE TROG

MAGICAL TREEHOUSE
WORD & ART IN CAHOOTS!

First published in Great Britain in 2017
By Magical Treehouse Publishing

Email: Info@MagicalTreehouse.com
www.MagicalTreehouse.com

A CIP catalogue record of this book is available from the British Library upon request.

ISBN 978-0-9956693-6-9 paperback

23441259R00024

Printed in Great Britain
by Amazon